Martin Luther King Jr.

A Photo-Illustrated Biography

by Kathy Feeney

Consultants:
Staff of the Martin Luther King Jr. National Historic Site

Bridgestone Books
an imprint of Capstone Press
Mankato, Minnesota

Bridgestone Books are published by Capstone Press
151 Good Counsel Drive, P.O. Box 669, Mankato, Minnesota 56002
http://www.capstone-press.com

Library of Congress Cataloging-in-Publication Data
Feeney, Kathy, 1954–
    Martin Luther King Jr.: a photo-illustrated biography/by Kathy Feeney.
    p.cm.—(Photo-illustrated biographies)
    Includes bibliographical references and index.
    Summary: A biography of the well-known minister, civil rights leader, and Nobel
Peace Prize winner who was assassinated in 1968.
    ISBN 0-7368-1111-7
    1. King, Martin Luther, Jr. 1929–1968—Juvenile literature. 2. King, Martin Luther, Jr.,
1929–1968—Pictorial works—Juvenile literature. 3. African Americans—United States—
Biography—Juvenile literature. 5. Baptists—United States—Clergy—Biography—Juvenile
literature. 6. African Americans—Civil rights—History—20th century—Juvenile literature.
[1. King, Martin Luther, Jr., 1929–1968. 2. Civil rights workers. 3. Clergy. 4. African
Americans—Biography.] I. Title. II. Series.
E185.97.K5 F44 2002
323'.092—dc21   2001005404

Editorial Credits
Gillia Olson, editor; Karen Risch, product planning editor; Timothy Halldin, cover
    designer; Steve Christensen, interior layout designer; Alta Schaffer, photo researcher

Photo Credits
Bettmann/CORBIS, 14, 18, 20
Boston University Photo Services, cover, 10, 12
Collection/CORBIS, 16
Flip Schulke/CORBIS, 8
Library of Congress, 6
National Archives, 4

The author wishes to dedicate this book to her friend, Jamarcus Bostick.

1 2 3 4 5 6 07 06 05 04 03 02

Table of Contents

Civil Rights Leader

Martin Luther King Jr. was a leader of the American Civil Rights movement. During the 1950s and 1960s, this movement helped African Americans gain the same rights as whites.

During Martin's lifetime, African Americans and whites were segregated. Laws in some states made African-American children and white children attend separate schools. Laws also separated whites and African Americans in public places such as theaters and restaurants.

The laws made it hard for African Americans to vote and to get a good education. The laws also limited job opportunities for African Americans. These laws are examples of racial discrimination.

Martin spent his life working for freedom and equality for all people. Martin hoped that one day all Americans would have equal rights.

Martin led many marches while working for equal rights for African Americans.

Childhood

Martin was born on January 15, 1929, in Atlanta, Georgia. Martin's mother was Alberta Williams King. She was a teacher. His father was Martin Luther King Sr. He was a minister at Ebenezer Baptist Church in Atlanta. Martin had an older sister named Willie Christine. His younger brother was Alfred Daniel. Martin's family called Martin by the nickname "M.L."

Martin went to Yonge Street Elementary school in Atlanta. The school was segregated. Every student at his school was African American. Martin was a good student. Martin could read before he entered first grade. He also was good at sports.

Martin spent a lot of time at his father's church. Martin liked listening to his father's sermons. He loved to sing along to hymns. He enjoyed learning about the Bible in Sunday school.

Martin grew up in this house near Ebenezer Baptist Church in Atlanta, Georgia.

"...let us see to it that increasingly...we give fair play and free opportunity for all people."
–Martin, during a high school speech, April 13, 1944

Education

Martin attended Booker T. Washington High School in Atlanta. He was a good athlete. Martin also was a very good student. His teachers allowed him to skip grades 9 and 12. He graduated from high school at age 15.

Martin then attended an African-American university in Atlanta called Morehouse College. He sang in the glee club and played on the football team. In high school, Martin wanted to become a doctor or a lawyer. But at Morehouse, he decided he wanted to become a minister. Martin felt he was called to help people through his faith in God.

Martin worked in factories and loaded trucks during summers. The hard labor made him understand the kinds of jobs most African Americans had.

Martin decided to become a minister while he was at Morehouse College. He later gave sermons at Ebenezer Baptist Church.

Learning Peace

After Morehouse, Martin enrolled in Crozer Seminary in Chester, Pennsylvania. He studied religion at this desegregated school. This was the first time he had attended a school with white students.

At the seminary, Martin learned about many religious leaders. He greatly respected Mohandas Gandhi of India. Gandhi changed unfair laws and freed India from Great Britain in 1947. He used peaceful protests instead of fighting.

Martin graduated from Crozer and earned the title of Reverend. Martin also received a scholarship to earn his doctorate at Boston University in Massachusetts. A doctorate is the highest degree someone can earn.

Martin met a student named Coretta Scott in Boston. Coretta studied music at the New England Conservatory of Music. Martin and Coretta married on June 18, 1953.

Martin met his wife Coretta while he was a student at Boston University.

The Reverend

In September 1954, Martin and Coretta moved to Montgomery, Alabama. Martin became a minister at Dexter Avenue Baptist Church. As a minister, Martin performed marriages and funeral services. He also gave people advice, visited the sick, helped the poor, and gave sermons.

Martin's schedule was very busy. But he continued to write his doctoral dissertation. This long report was the final requirement to receive his doctorate. In June 1955, Martin received his doctorate from Boston University. He now was Dr. King.

Martin and Coretta lived in a large white house close to the church. Martin and Coretta had four children. They named them Yolanda Denise, Martin Luther III, Dexter Scott, and Bernice Albertine.

Martin graduated from Boston University in 1955.

"Right here in Montgomery, when the history books are written in the future, somebody will have to say, 'There lived...a people who had the moral courage to stand up for their rights.'"
–Martin, speech during a meeting of the Montgomery Improvement Association, December 5, 1955

Peaceful Protests

Montgomery's city buses were segregated. Whites sat in the front seats. African Americans sat in the back seats. On December 1, 1955, African-American Rosa Parks rode home on a city bus. She sat just behind the seats for whites.

The crowded bus stopped to pick up a white passenger. Rosa was told to give up her seat and stand. Rosa was tired. She had spent long hours on her feet at work. She refused. The bus driver found a police officer. Rosa was arrested and taken to jail.

Rosa's courage inspired Martin. He and others in Montgomery protested the bus segregation laws. They organized a boycott. African Americans in Montgomery refused to ride the city buses. Their peaceful protest lasted 381 days.

People also brought a lawsuit against the bus company. On December 20, 1956, the U.S. Supreme Court ruled that segregation on city buses was illegal.

Martin admired Rosa Parks' courage. They are pictured here at an event 10 years after the boycott.

"I have a dream that my four children will one day live in a nation where they will not be judged by the color of their skin but by the content of their character."
–Martin, during the March on Washington, August 28, 1963

Famous Speaker

After the Montgomery bus boycott, Martin moved his family to Atlanta. He worked with his father at Ebenezer Baptist Church. Martin also founded the Southern Christian Leadership Conference. This group's members challenged racial segregation.

Martin had a gift for public speaking. He gave one of his greatest speeches on August 28, 1963, in Washington, D.C. More than 250,000 Americans had come to march in support of a civil rights bill. This bill would end racial segregation in public places. It also would make it a crime to deny jobs and education opportunities to African Americans.

Martin gave his famous "I Have a Dream" speech during the march. He talked about his dream for racial equality. The march and Martin's speech led Congress to pass the Civil Rights Act on July 2, 1964.

Martin gave his "I Have a Dream" speech in front of more than 250,000 people.

"I...believe that peoples everywhere can have three meals a day for their bodies, education and culture for their minds, and dignity, equality, and freedom for their spirts."
–Martin, during his Nobel Peace Prize acceptance speech, December 10, 1964

Nobel Peace Prize

Martin's method of working for equal rights through peaceful means was recognized. In 1964, Martin received the Nobel Peace Prize. The Nobel Committee presents this award each year. It goes to the person who has done the most toward gaining world peace.

Martin, his wife, and his parents flew to Norway for the award ceremony. On December 10, 1964, Martin received the Nobel Peace Prize at Oslo University. At age 35, Martin became the youngest person ever to receive the award.

In his acceptance speech, Martin said the prize did not belong only to him. It was meant for all people "who love peace and brotherhood." He received a medal and $54,600 in prize money. Martin donated most of the money to civil rights groups.

Martin received the Nobel Peace Prize in Norway.

Martin's Death

People sometimes disagreed with Martin's ideas about equal rights. During peaceful protests, people threw rocks at Martin. He often was sent to jail. His house was bombed in 1956.

In early April 1968, Martin went to Memphis, Tennessee, to support African-American garbage workers. They wanted fairer wages and better working conditions. He and other civil rights leaders were staying at the Lorraine Motel. On April 4, Martin went onto the balcony outside his room for a break. James Earl Ray shot and killed Martin as he stood on the balcony.

Thousands of people went to Martin's funeral in Atlanta. Millions more watched on TV. His grave is now part of a National Historic site. Americans celebrate his life on the third Monday in January. Martin Luther King Jr. Day became an official national holiday in 1986.

Thousands of people marched behind Martin's coffin after his funeral.

Fast Facts about Martin Luther King Jr.

 Martin first learned about racism when two white boys said they could not play with Martin because he was African-American.

 Martin Jr.'s and Martin Sr.'s names originally were Michael. Martin Sr. decided to change them in honor of religious leader Martin Luther.

 During a signing for his book *Stride Toward Freedom*, a woman stabbed Martin in the chest with a letter opener.

Dates in Martin Luther King Jr.'s Life

1929—Martin is born on January 15 in Atlanta, Georgia.

1935—Enters first grade at Yonge Street Elementary

1944—Enters Morehouse College in Atlanta

1948—Enters Crozer Theological Seminary in Chester, Pennsylvania

1953—Marries Coretta Scott

1954—Named minister of Dexter Avenue Baptist Church

1955—Receives doctorate and leads Montgomery bus boycott

1960—Becomes co-minster of Ebenezer Baptist Church with his father

1963—Gives "I Have a Dream" speech in Washington, D.C., on August 28

1964—Wins the Nobel Peace Prize

1968—Shot and killed in Memphis, Tennessee, on April 4

Words to Know

boycott (BOI-kot)—a protest where people refuse to use or buy something

discrimination (diss-krim-i-NAY-shuhn)—treating people unfairly because of their race, country of birth, or gender

glee club (GLEE KLUHB)—a choir that usually sings short songs

minister (MIN-uh-stur)—the leader of a Christian church group who leads religious ceremonies

scholarship (SKOL-ur-ship)—money that pays for someone to go to college or to follow a course of study

segregate (SEG-ruh-gate)—to separate or keep people apart from the main group

seminary (SEM-uh-ner-ee)—a school that trains students to become ministers, priests, or rabbis

sermon (SUR-muhn)—a speech given during a religious service

Read More

Adler, David A. *Dr. Martin Luther King, Jr.* New York: Holiday House, 2001.

Rappaport, Doreen. *Martin's Big Words: The Life of Martin Luther King, Jr.* New York: Hyperion Books for Children, 2001.

Summer, L. S. *The March on Washington.* Journey to Freedom. Chanhassen, Minn.: Child's World, 2001.

Useful Addresses

**Birmingham Civil
Rights Institute**
520 Sixteenth Street North
Birmingham, AL 35203

**Southern Christian Leadership
Conference**
334 Auburn Avenue NE
Atlanta, GA 30312

Internet Sites

Dexter Avenue Baptist Church
http://www.cr.nps.gov/nr/travel/civilrights/al7.htm
Martin Luther King Jr. National Historic Site
http://www.nps.gov/malu/home.htm
The National Civil Rights Museum
http://216.157.9.6/civilrights/main.htm

Index